ESCAPE!

THE MATH MAZE

SOLVE YOUR WAY OUT!

CODE

ACCESS DENIED!

Alix Wood

Use your **MATH** skills to **ESCAPE!**

Gareth Stevens
PUBLISHING

Please visit our website, www.garethstevens.com. For a free color catalog of all our high-quality books, call toll free 1-800-542-2595 or fax 1-877-542-2596.

Cataloging-in-Publication Data
Names: Wood, Alix.
Title: The math maze: solve your way out! / Alix Wood.
Description: New York : Gareth Stevens, 2023. | Series: Escape!
Identifiers: ISBN 9781538277331 (pbk.) | ISBN 9781538277355 (library bound) | ISBN 9781538277348 (6 pack) | ISBN 9781538277362 (ebook)
Subjects: LCSH: Puzzles--Juvenile literature. | Problem solving--Juvenile literature. | Logic puzzles--Juvenile literature. | Mathematics--Juvenile literature.
Classification: LCC GV1493.W663 2023 | DDC 793.73--dc23

Produced for Gareth Stevens Publishing by Alix Wood Books
Designed and Illustrated by Alix Wood
Editor: Eloise Macgregor

Printed in the United States of America

CPSIA compliance information: Batch # CSGS23 For further information contact Gareth Stevens, New York, New York at 1-800-542-2595.

Next to the park stands a large house. The owner, Mrs. Mwangi, is a math professor at the university. She has two passions: math and gardening. Mrs. Mwangi does not welcome people in her garden. A large wall and a heavy iron gate help guard her property. So, it is a bit of a disaster when you accidentally kick your new soccer ball over the wall!

You can just see your ball through the ironwork. Surely, you could grab it and run out without being noticed! You try the gate, and to your surprise, it is unlocked. But as you grab the ball, you hear the gate slam and lock behind you. That was a mistake! How are you going to get out now? The gate has some strange shapes cut into the metalwork. The words "puzzle your way out" are engraved in the stone archway.

HOW TO ESCAPE!

Use your math knowledge to puzzle your way out of the math maze. Solve puzzles to get the codes you need to open a series of locked boxes. Each box contains one shaped key. You need all the shapes to open the door and escape. All the information you need to solve the puzzles can be found in this book. The answer to a puzzle on one page may be found on other pages or in the notebook.

Get stuck? Answers and hints can be found at the back of this book.

THE PATH

Your ball came to rest next to a small locked box. Nearby, there is a scrap of paper. It has some numbers and squares on it. Some of the paper has been torn away. Puzzle your way out? Perhaps you need to solve this puzzle to get a shaped key from that box!

$$x - 2 = 4$$

THE STONES

Some large inscribed stones stand near the locked gate. Holes in the ground make you think some of the stones are missing. A safe is embedded in the wall. It has numbers and math symbols on the three dials. A ramp leads up to a wooden platform.

THE PAVED AREA

Looking down from the bridge, you can see an area of numbered paving stones. An arrow made from pebbles points to one of the slabs. Is that the start of a maze? A scrap of striped paper lies next to a locked safe. The safe needs four numbers . . . but which four? You shake your head in despair.

THE ROPE BRIDGE

At one end of the platform, you see a padlocked suitcase. Perhaps there is a key hidden in there? But what are the three shapes you need to open it? A rope bridge leads to another platform. It looks pretty dangerous. Some of the planks are missing.

THE MAZE

A maze decorated with math problems appears below you. At the exit of the maze, there is a locked trunk. You need four numbers to open the lock. Near the steps, you find a book. It looks helpful.

Follow the correct path!

```
                                    2
    ÷  9 = 5   +  4 = 2   x  9 = 17  -
    3           3          4          8
    = 3         = 6        = 6        11
    x  3 = 8   x  1 = 5   ÷  2 = 4   +
    2           2          3          1
    = 6         = 10       = 7        13
    +  2 = 8   +  2 = 11  -  5 = 12  -
    3           1          4          5
    = 4         = 9        = 6        = 7
    x  1 = 5   -  5 = 7   +  1 = 1   ÷
                = 9
                = 0
```

MATH NOTEBOOK

this book belongs to
Professor Mwangi

Spaces can be shapes too!

MATH NOTES

Sudoku

In a 4 x 4 sudoku puzzle grid, each row and each column adds up to **10**. The numbers 1, 2, 3, and 4 occur only once in each column and once in each row. You have to work out what the missing numbers are.

this number must be a 3

Each 4-number square adds up to 10 too.

2		4	1
	4		3
4	1		
3	2	1	4

this number must be a 1

Can you work out the rest?

Logic math puzzles

Can you work out what each symbol stands for? You should have all the information you need.

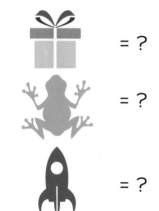

🎁 + 🎁 + 🎁 = 18   🎁 = ?

🎁 × 🐸 = 12   🐸 = ?

🎁 + 🐸 + 🚀 = 18   🚀 = ?

Probability

Probability is the chance that something will happen. If we toss a coin, it could be heads or tails. So, the chance of throwing a head has the probability of one chance out of two.

There are six possible numbers when you toss a dice. So, each number has a one in six chance of being thrown. What's the probability of throwing an even number? There are three even numbers: two, four, and six. So, your chance of throwing an even number is three out of six.

Odd and Even

Even numbers end in 2, 4, 6, 8, and 0.
Odd numbers end in 1, 3, 5, 7, and 9.

Just even!

DATTATREYA RAMCHANDRA KAPREKAR was an Indian mathematician and schoolteacher who discovered the Kaprekar's Constant. Almost any four-digit number will produce exactly the same four-digit number after, at most, 7 steps!

I love this guy!

KAPREKAR'S CONSTANT

Step 1: Write down four numbers.
At least one of the numbers must be different from the others.

Step 2: Sort the four numbers so they make the biggest number possible. So 5381 would become 8531.

Step 3: Now sort your numbers into the smallest number they can make, for example 1358.

Step 4: Subtract the smallest number from the biggest number.

Repeat Step 2 to Step 4 with the result.
Then repeat . . . and repeat . . .

After seven steps at most, the same four numbers will just keep repeating, no matter what numbers you started with!

try it!

$d + 3 = 4$ What's d? Can you work it out? $1+3=4$, so d must be 1. Algebra is a part of math where letters or symbols represent numbers. It's fun to work out what the letters stand for.

Prime numbers

Prime numbers are special numbers. They can only be divided by 1 and themselves.

3 is a prime number.
9 is not a prime number because it can be divided by 3 as well as itself and 1.

The number 1 is not a prime number. Why? Because itself and 1 are the same number. They need to be different for it to be a prime number.

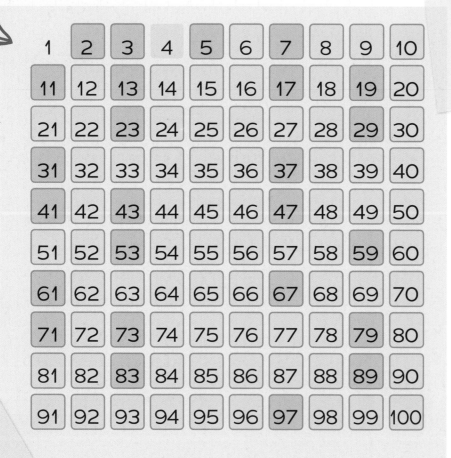

Many prime numbers end in 1, 3, 7, or 9.

They never end in 4, **6**, **8**, or 0.

A	B	C	D	E	F	G	H	I	J	K	L	M
4	5	6	7	8	9	10	11	12	13	14	15	16

Sending Coded Messages

To make a message hard to read, you can use numbers as letters. A secret key can show what letter each number stands for. The person that sends the message and the one that gets it need to know the key.

Circles and Degrees

Every circle can be divided into 360 units called degrees (°). Why 360? Ancient mathematicians noticed Earth took about 360 days to circle around the sun. So, they decided to divide circles into 360 degrees!

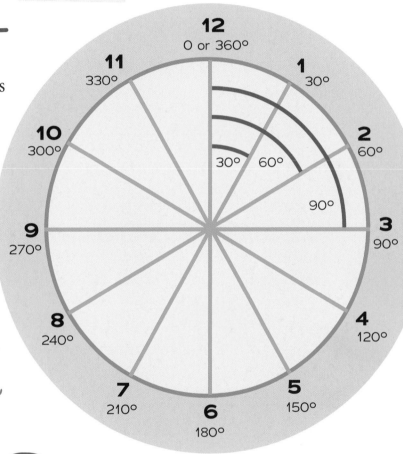

Each hour segment on a clock is 30 degrees. So, 3 o'clock would be 3 units of 30. That is, 90 degrees.

Half past three?

The minute hand would point at the 6, which is at 180 degrees. The hour hand would point halfway between 3 and 4. Half of 30 is 15. So the hour hand would point to 105 degrees (90 plus 15).

N	O	P	Q	R	S	T	U	V	W	X	Y	Z
17	18	19	20	21	22	23	24	25	26	1	2	3

The Fibonacci Sequence

Leonardo Fibonacci was a mathematician from Pisa, Italy. He discovered this math sequence now named after him.

Starting with 0 and 1, every number is the sum of the two numbers before it.

0, 1, 2, 3

Add the first two numbers, so 0 plus 1 is 1. Then 1 added to 1 is 2; 2 added to 1 is 3; and so on.

Can you work out the missing number below?

0, 1, 1, 2, 3,___, 8

0, 1, 1, 2, 3, 5, 8, 13, 21, 34, 55, 89, 144, 233, 377, 610, 987, 1597, 2584, 4181, 6765, 10946, 17711, 28657, 46368, 75025, 121393, 196418, 317811

THE LOCKED SHED

At the bottom of the steps, there is a locked shed.
X, y, and z? Is that algebra?

IN THE SHED

Inside the shed, you see a locked brown chest with a number keypad. A confusing note is taped to the door. It looks as though it may be in some kind of code. There is a number keypad on the chest. It needs four numbers to open it.

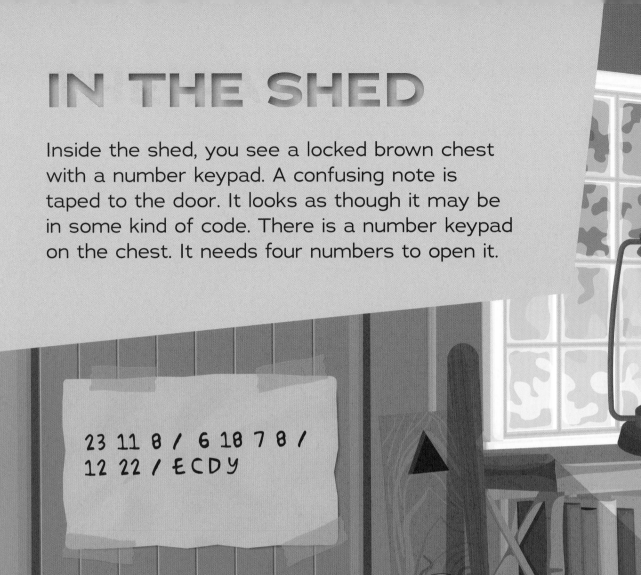

THE TABLE

On the small table, you see some math notes.
A safe and a calculator lie next to them.
Maybe the notes hold a clue to the four
numbers you need? Constant puzzles!
When will it end?

$$8531$$
$$-1358$$

?

THE WORKSHOP

You leave the shed and head into the next door. The workshop is a muddle of clutter. A clock lies broken on the floor. It is not obvious if there is a safe here. And if there is a safe, how might you open it? Time will tell.

Remember:
Minute hand 180
Hour hand 75

45

THE CASINO TABLE

In a corner of the workshop, a green table is set up like a casino. Is she a gambler? I guess being great at math might make some games less of a gamble. A red light is flashing on the roulette wheel. Notes and books are scattered about on the table.

How likely that I will roll a 3?
? out of 6

How likely I'll roll an odd number?
? out of 6

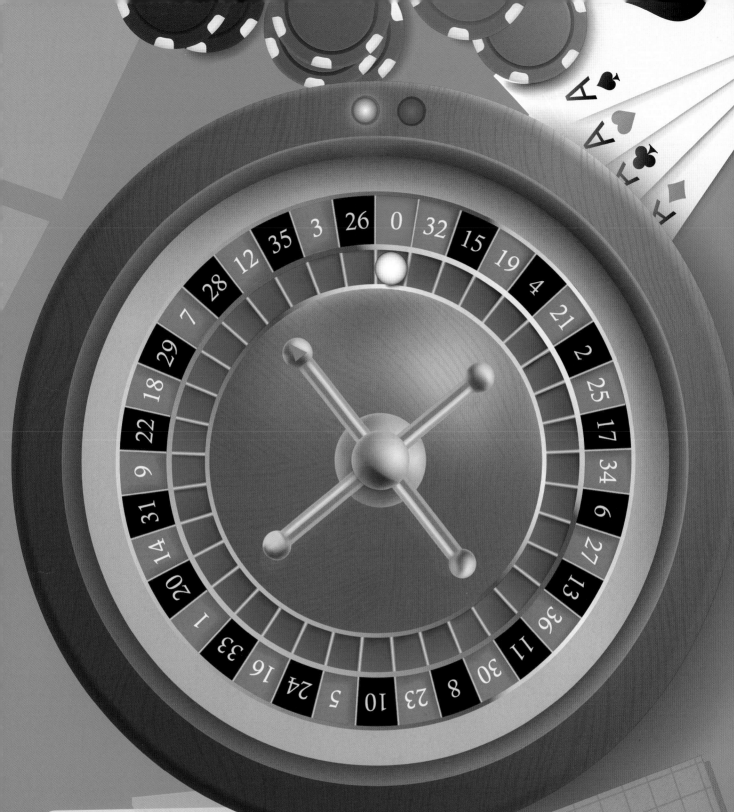

How likely I'll spin a red number? ? out of 37

PROBABILITY HANDBOOK

GEOMETRY

It is bright outside in the daylight. Just one more key to find and you can get out of here. Maybe it is in that trunk? There are shapes on the keypad. Triangles, circles, and squares . . .

Did you escape the math maze?
Check your answers on page 32.

HINTS

The Path
1. Search the book for the rest of the paper puzzle.
2. You may find some help in the notebook.
3. Find the missing numbers that go in the colored squares. Then enter them in color order on the keypad.

The Stones
1. Can you find more inscribed stones in the book?
2. Work out which of the numbers and symbols might make the sum equal 9.
3. The correct numbers or symbols in order from left to right will open the safe.

The Paved Area
1. Shake your head and look at the striped note. It may give a clue.
2. Look in the notebook for information on prime numbers.
3. Follow the prime numbers through the maze. Are any in circles?

The Rope Bridge
1. Can you find the missing planks?
2. The numbers on the bridge follow a sequence.
3. Find the right planks and line up their shapes in order on the padlock.

The Maze
1. Does 2 x 4 equal 6? The right path has the right answers.
2. Collect all the correct answers. Some are odd, and some are even.
3. Check the notebook for a clue how to get to just four numbers.

The Locked Shed
1. Search the book for x, y, and z.
2. Learn about solving algebra in the notebook.
3. Enter the values for x, y, and z.

In the Shed
1. See if you can work out the coded note.
2. Look in the notebook for help.
3. Numbers can be letters, and letters can be numbers.

The Table
1. To solve this puzzle, you can start with just about ANY four numbers!

2. Kaprekar? Who is that?
3. Try subtracting the big number from the small one until the same number keeps repeating. That number is your code.

The Workshop
1. That clock is a circle.
2. All circles can be divided into degrees.
3. The note on the wall will help you find out the time. The time is the code.

The Casino Table
1. Gambling is all about probability.
2. Can you find useful information in the notebook?
3. Answer the questions on the scraps of paper to get the code.

Geometry
1. How many of each shape can you see?
2. Spaces can make shapes too.
3. Four squares together form a square. Triangles can be similar.

ANSWERS A mirror will help you read these answers.

6-7: 4322; the missing circled sudoku numbers, in color order

8-9: 7-3; the missing stones make up the sum 5+7-3=9

10-11: 7237; follow the prime numbers through the maze; the code numbers are circled: 7, 2, 37

12-13: ● ▲ ★ ; the shapes on the planks 1, 8, and 55; numbers from the Fibonacci sequence

14-15: 4680; the results of the correct sums in the maze were 4936890; the even numbers were 4680

20-21: 675; x is 6 (6-2 = 4), y is 7 (7+5=12), z is 5 (5-4=1)

22-23: 8672; the numbers for the letters from the code cypher

24-25: 6174; Kaprekar's constant

26-27: 230; the clock is the safe; 2:30 is where the hands would point to at 180 and 75 degrees

28-29: 1318; the probabilities are 1 chance out of 6, 3 chances out of 6, and 18 chances out of 37

30-31: 5914; 5 triangles, 9 circles, and 14 squares (the spaces form triangles and circles too, and four tiles and nine tiles make up more squares)

32